ROADS

The Non-Profit's Quick Guide for

Gaining the Commitment

By

Bryan H. Nelson

ISBN: 1453804064

ISBN - 13: 9781453804063

Library of Congress Cataloging-in-Publication Data

TABLE OF CONTENTS

ROADS

The Non-Profit's Quick Guide for

Gaining the Commitment

CHAPTER 1

An Overview of ROADS

Mission-driven, non-profit organizations rely upon relationships with community supporters to achieve their goals and realize their mission. *ROADS: The Non-Profit's Quick Guide for Gaining the Commitment* outlines a systematic approach to move volunteers, donors, and funders from *potential* prospects to *active* and fully *engaged supporters* of your organization.

While very large mission-driven organizations attract board members and donors due to the prestige of being associated with these groups, smaller, less visible non-profits often struggle to meet their ongoing needs:

- Program/Activity Volunteers

- Board Members

- Donors

- Sponsors

- Funders

Attracting, recruiting, and retaining ongoing volunteer, donor, and funder commitments is critical for long-term success. Borrowing from successful professional marketing and sales practices, non-profit organizations can create a strategic and systematic approach to attract and retain these supporters.

The key to converting community members to fully engaged and committed supporters is implementing a relational selling process. The relational selling process used in the business world, with adaptation, is appropriate and effective for non-profit organizations. In the business world, it is used to align services and products with the needs or perceived needs of the customers. The same selling process used by non-profit organizations will align their relationships with their supporters. For non-profits, the selling process becomes the process of *gaining the commitment*. The key question for every non-profit organization becomes:

> *How can we effectively gain and retain supporters of our organization?*

The three primary outcomes non-profit organizations must accomplish in the recruiting process are:

- the creation of an organizational relationship with the prospect,

- full understanding of the prioritized needs and/or requirements of the prospect, and

- assurance you have met at least one of the prospect's needs.

When these outcomes are achieved, they will result in a higher success rate in gaining the commitment.

> **Focus:** ROADS is not an assigned sales process. It is a systematic approach for gaining the commitment of a prospective volunteer, donor or funder. This is an approach that can be adopted throughout your organization; by the executive director, by the board members and by the staff members, to assure a consistent method for recruiting and retaining your organization's supporters.

A non-profit organization should adopt a marketing or sales process that closely aligns with developing relationships. The ROADS process of gaining the commitment is fully adaptable to the *values*, *mission*, and *goals* of working with and serving the community.

This process is *not a*:

- high pressure sales technique,

- "quick sales" close,

- hit-or-miss sales process, or

- "cold" approach.

This process is:

- focused upon relationship-building,

• an established and successful process for gaining new supporters,

• a way to establish a win-win relationship for the organization and the supporter, and

• adaptable to any set of program or service offerings of the organization.

Before discussing the process, a review of the terms used in this guide is necessary.

> For non-profits, the selling process becomes the process of gaining the commitment. ROADS is the systematic approach which allows non-profit organizations to enhance their success rate in gaining the commitment.

CHAPTER 2

Clarifying Terms

The following terms are used in describing the ROADS process throughout this guide.

Volunteers

These individuals provide direct program or activity-based support, and include members of the board of directors.

Donors

These are individuals, businesses, organizations, and/or estates that provide direct cash donations, sponsorships, and/or endowments.

Funders

These are entities that provide direct funding to organizations, including governmental, charitable trusts, and foundations, through an "application" process.

Prospect

This generic term refers to any individual or group interested in becoming actively engaged with the organization. Prospects include *volunteers*, *donors*, and *funders*.

Supporters

These are individuals and groups with whom you have gained the commitment to become actively engaged with your organization.

Marketing/Telling the Story

In the business world, *marketing* and *selling* are well defined. Many non-profit organizations shy from these terms. The concepts, however, are critical for the non-profit community to embrace.

Marketing is a broad-based approach intended to gain interest in the company's offerings. It is informational and intended to create "name brand recognition," as well as knowledge of the company's products and services. In the non-profit world, *telling the story* is marketing. The telling of the story comes in different forms and formats, from Web sites to brochures to events, non-profits engage in *telling the story* (marketing) every day.

Selling/Gaining the Commitment

In the business sector, closing the sale is the end-game goal. For the non-profit community, the end-game goal is to *gain* and *retain* the commitment of volunteers, donors, and funders, as well as clients. The ability to gain the commitment can be hit-or-miss if the process is not implemented effectively. Some commitments are never achieved; some are achieved for a short time, while precious few become long-term.

A final note...

The "selling," or gaining the commitment, process is ongoing. It should not stop if the intent is to *retain the new supporter*. Gaining the initial commitment is just the first step in retaining the commitment over time.

CHAPTER 3

The **ROADS** Process

R *Relationship* building (personal and organizational) with your prospective volunteer, donor, or funding source

O *Organize* the prospects needs and talents. (Highest priority for prospect)

A *Articulate* the prospect's needs back to him/her. (Use feedback to assure understanding of those needs/outcomes.)

D *Document* the next steps in completing the gaining the commitment process.

S *Seek* ongoing feedback from the new client or supporter. This is the first step in retaining the commitment.

Focus: ROADS is a process which allows members of a non-profit organization to enhance their ability to gain commitments from individuals and entities who can provide support for their organization.

Each step in ROADS builds upon the next. Each step moves the potential prospect to an active prospect, and then to a committed supporter. The final step, **S**eek feedback, is essential in maintaining the relationship over time. In the for-profit world, it is well established that retaining the client is exponentially less expensive and time consuming than developing new clients. The same is true for non-profit organizations.

Sales, or gaining the commitment, processes are "learned" techniques. While some people are born sales people, many people find selling a less-than-desirable activity. Anyone can learn to implement a relational sales process. This process does not require a certain type of personality. This process relies upon making a connection with a prospective supporter. It is a process that is conversational. It is a process that is documented. It is a process that works.

The process of creating relationships as a method of gaining the commitment is a typical value held by mission-driven organizations. The process ROADS uses allows any member of a mission-driven organization to incorporate a "sales process" into their relationship building processes they currently use to serve their clients.

For non-profit organizations, which derive a portion of their revenues from "fee-for-service" programs, the ROADS process is an effective method of gaining the commitment of clients. While the focus of ROADS is on gaining the commitment of supporters, this process can also help an organization gain more clients. To reiterate an earlier comment, ROADS is a relationship-based process. This process respects the needs and desires of the person you wish to be engaged with in your organization. At times, that person may be a client, rather than a supporter.

CHAPTER 4

Relationship Building

Relationship Building

O

A

D

S

Non-profit organizations build **R**elationships every day. The relationship process you use should align with the mission, values, and goals of your organization. Personal relationships are important in establishing trust. Building organizational trust during this step in ROADS is critical. Engaging in relationship-building allows the prospect to understand the organization more clearly. It also begins the process of building trust that the organization will value the supporter's participation and commitment to it.

The goal in building a successful relationship is to create *long-term relationships* with the organization itself, not the individuals within the organization. To this end, as staff members and volunteers engage in this stage of the gaining commitment process, it is essential to focus on building the *organizational trust* with the prospect.

> **Focus:** During this phase, your "telling the story" (marketing) is narrowed, as you begin to listen to your prospective volunteer, donor or funder's interests and/or requirements.

This stage is the time of *listening more and talking less.* One of the goals in this stage is to learn *why* someone is taking the time to meet with you. Has he/she heard the organization's story, a story of its great work, or does he/she have personal knowledge of someone the organization has assisted? Ask the question and then listen. Ask about what drives the person. Then listen. To maximize your prospective supporter's answers, use broad open-ended questions/statements, such as:

> • *Tell me what you know about our organization. (then listen)*

> • *What part or parts of our mission/services/ programs are most exciting or compelling to you? (then listen)*

> • *What types of things do you do to be involved in the community/with this part of our community/etc.? (then listen)*

14

As your prospect describes his/her interests, experiences, or requirements, you may learn of one or more areas in which he/she could provide much needed support. Your prospect will learn that you have a sincere interest in meeting his/her needs, and are not just filling a need for your organization. This is the essence of relationship building.

Individuals will engage with the organization to meet both the needs of the organization and their needs. Everyone working on behalf of the organization to recruit new supporters must understand that until the prospect's need(s) are met, the organization itself simply will not be enough to achieve a "gained commitment." By understanding and directly working on achieving your prospect's needs, you greatly enhance your success rate in successfully recruiting new supporters.

> The **R**elationship Building Phase begins to move the potential prospect to an active prospect. Both of you are identifying shared interests and needs which could be mutually met if a gained commitment was achieved.

CHAPTER 5

Organize the Prospect's Priorities

R

Organize the Prospect's Priorities

A

D

S

This is the "drilling down phase" of gaining the commitment. The process of **O**rganizing your prospect's priorities may be straightforward, or it may be more random. An individual who has a great deal of knowledge about the organization may be interested in a very specific role, or set of roles, which are readily articulated. For this type of prospect, the priorities may be clearly delineated and organized.

For individuals who know little, yet are interested in learning more about the organization, active listening and *key question asking* will be required. These individuals may come into your initial meeting with only a vague idea about the organization and how they might be able to support it. As you are working to build the relationship, they may learn of additional aspects of the organization that drive them to learn more about the "what's" and the "how's" of the organization. As your prospect shares interests in various programs or areas in which he/she could serve, you should begin to organize this list of interest areas. When this occurs, the interviewer needs to be ready to address all areas which might be a fit for the prospect. By asking probing questions and then describing how those roles are accomplished, you and the prospective supporter move closer to understanding each other's interests and needs.

> **Focus:** During this phase, your goal is to have a "draft list" of the prospect's priorities in becoming a supporter of your organization. To fully achieve that goal, a written list should be developed.

Organizing a prospect's priorities means just that; organizing them in *writing*. Now is not the time to finalize the list. It is, however, important to list out the priorities as you understand them. Remember, you understand the prioritized *needs* of your organization, so you now must be able to align the prospect's highest priorities with the organization's needs.

Organizing your prospect's stated interests in your non-profit is critical to better understanding how best to match your needs with the prospect's stated interests. This list is certainly not set in stone; however, it sets the stage for the next step in the ROADS process. Until you have a reasonable idea of the needs of your prospect, you have little chance of aligning his/her stated interests and desires with the needs of your non-profit.

> The **O**rganization phase is one that allows the interviewer to better understand where the prospective supporter's needs and desires are best aligned with the organization's needs and mission.

CHAPTER 6

Articulate the Prospect's Priorities

R

O

Articulate the Prospect's Priorites

D

S

This is the "sorting and clarifying" phase of gaining the commitment. As your prospect reveals his/her priorities, you now have information you need for clarifying those priorities. This sorting and clarifying process is crucial if alignment is to be established between the needs of your prospect and the needs of your organization.

The real power of this stage of ROADS is that your prospect has heard his/her needs reflected back to him/her. The first step in any trust building process is to know your interests are being met. Articulating the needs of the prospect in a prioritized way further builds trust.

> **Focus:** During this phase your goal is to articulate, clarify and agree on the highest priorities your prospect has in working with your organization.

Articulating your understanding of the prospect's needs may be done in a conversational way, or in a listing of "heard" priorities. Either way, the message you are providing your prospect is that you heard him/her, you are sincerely interested in meeting his/her needs, and that those needs would be a great match for your organization.

When a prospect expresses several ways he/she would like to engage with the organization, articulating back those interests is important. Your goal in gaining the commitment is to assure your prospect that his/her highest priority interests will be met. The best method for assuring clarity with your prospect is to *ask* for clarification.

Clarification statements or questions can include:

• *I heard you say…. Is that correct?*

• *When you spoke about…, how might that match with [donating to, working in, joining our board, etc.]?*

• *It sounded like your biggest interest is….*

• *Have I missed any of the areas in which you might be interested in working with our organization?*

The **A**rticulating phase better assures gaining the commitment because you are engaging the prospect in the most critical area of their needs. You also now clearly understand how the prospect's needs align with the needs of the organization.

Successfully articulating the prospect's interests and desires, and then aligning those with the organization's needs, leads you to the next phase of ROADS.

CHAPTER 7

Document the Next Steps

R

O

A

Document the Next Steps

S

This is the gaining the commitment stage of the process. By **D**ocumenting the next steps, you formalize that commitment. Your prospect has agreed to become a volunteer, a donor, a funder, or a combination of these roles. He or she is now an actively engaged *supporter*. Gaining the commitment has to be documented with enough detail to assure that each entity understands his/her commitment and his/her responsibilities.

Documenting the specific role or roles your new supporter has agreed upon assures several key outcomes.

The supporter clearly knows *what* he/she will be doing.

The supporter understands *how* "on-boarding" into your organization will take place.

The supporter knows *who* will be his/her next contact in your organization.

Keep in mind that the documentation phase is critical organizationally. Everyone in your organization engaged in the gaining the commitment process must document the *what, how, and who* your new supporter will engage with next. It is essential that the documentation process is systematized to assure long-term success in attracting and retaining new supporters.

> **Focus:** During this phase your goal is to document the commitment made, and assure that your new supporter understands what they will be doing, and who will be their next contact within the organization.

The documentation phase is vital for assuring that your new supporter understands the process for his/her initial engagement with the organization. It also creates a paper trail, which provides accountability within the organization. The only way to assure consistency in any process or procedure is to hold employees and board members accountable for following the procedure. This phase in the ROADS process provides the necessary accountability trail to better assure consistent success in gainlny the commitment and successful engagement with the organization.

The documentation stage is very important in assuring your new supporter will be supported as he/she begin working with your organization. The documentation phase also provides an accountability trail, to assure the organization's staff and board members will successfully carry through with commitments made to the new supporter. Documentation reduces the risk of letting these new valuable assets slip through the cracks.

> The **D**ocumentation stage is not the final step in the process. It is the step that allows both the new supporter and the organization to move from gained commitment to gained engagement.

The final phase of ROADS is the first phase of *retaining the commitment*. You have now successfully "closed the sale" and achieved your desired outcome. Now is not the time to sit on your laurels. The final section of this guide discusses the crucial process of retaining this valuable new resource for your organization.

CHAPTER 8

Seek Feedback

R

O

A

D

Seek Feedback

This is the final stage of gaining the commitment and the first phase of *retaining the commitment.* Businesses understand how much more effective and efficient it is to *retain* a customer than to recruit and gain a new one. That same principle applies to gaining and then retaining the commitment of a supporter in a non-profit organization. When you achieve your goal—a gained commitment—it is extraordinarily efficient for the organization to retain that commitment over time.

This is not the time to relax, enjoy the success of adding another supporter, and move forward. To retain volunteers, board members, donors, and funders successfully, the organization must systematically work to seek the appropriate feedback to assure the supporters' needs are consistently being met.

The goal of the organization is to determine how best to capture the feedback necessary to retain its supporters. Some of the feedback loops established will be straightforward and dictated by the supporter (e.g., funder), while other feedback systems may need to be more creative and take more time to develop.

Focus: During this phase you must create and implement a set of feedback processes that each type of supporter needs to assure that their needs/requirement are being met over time.

Whether it is human nature, lack of time, or organizational complacency, continuing to seek feedback often falls short. Without seeking feedback, the organization risks several negative outcomes over time:

• A loss of enthusiasm by the supporter to remain engaged with the organization

• A lost opportunity to increase the amount of engagement by the supporter

• A complete loss of commitment

The outcome of seeking feedback is to assure ongoing alignment between your supporter and your organization. There is no one feedback system that will be able to capture the information your organization needs over time. Creativity and persistence in seeking feedback is required.

Organizations should create a series of questions and comments focused in each of the supporter areas that will allow them to create the feedback systems they need. These questions and comments may include:

For Board Members:

• *Why do you continue to serve on our board of directors?*

• *What aspect(s) of board membership do you enjoy? Which ones do you not enjoy?*

• *Do you have an interest in leading a committee, becoming an officer, or leading a specific task force?*

• *What other areas of the organization would you like to engage with?*

For Program/Services Volunteers:

• *Tell us what you enjoy about working in xyz program.*

• *Are there other programs you would like to learn more about?*

• *How can we make your experience with us more enjoyable/rewarding?*

• Would you like to consider…(joining our board of directors/working at XXX event/ donating to the organization/etc.)?

For Donors:

• We were able to use your generous donation to…. Are there other areas of our organization that you would like to make sure are addressed with any future donations you make to us?

• What other information can we provide you to help you in making decisions in the future about donating to our organization?

• How else would you like to participate in our organization?

• Do you have family members, friends, or business associates who might like to participate in our organization in some way?

The Seek Feedback phase is the first step in retaining the commitment. In Seeking the feedback, the process should produce a re-commitment through

Relating
Organizing
Articulating, and
Documenting

the supporter's interests, desires and/or regulatory requirement in working with your organization over time.

CHAPTER 9

Conclusion

ROADS uses the same relational sales processes successfully implemented by businesses, but it adapts them to the needs of the non-profit sector. These processes are strategic, they are applied systemically throughout an organization, and they are used to gain and retain the commitment of volunteers, donors, and funders—the supporters of an organization.

Mission-driven organizations engage people to accomplish their mission and goals. The strength of ROADS is the alignment of its *people-focused process* with an organization's *people-focused* services and programs. When the gaining commitment process is fully aligned with an organization's primary method of conducting business, the selling system is natural and more readily achieved.

To assist the reader, a Gaining the Commitment Checklist can be found in the following section. The checklist provides a template to document the steps of the relational selling process. For individuals new to relational sales, this checklist can be used as a step-by-step guide. Learning any new skill can feel awkward.

But by using this checklist, the interviewer can move through each of the phases of ROADS, documenting the prospect's stated needs and desires.

The second use for this checklist is to ensure that a paper trail is created. This checklist can be particularly useful as the hand off is made from the interviewer to the next person in the organization, who will begin engaging the new supporter with his/her desired role(s).

Creating a set process of Gaining the Commitment results in establishing an effective and efficient system of adding valuable resources for an organization. The Gaining the Commitment Checklist becomes the initial stage of creating your new system.

For organizations interested in enhancing their ability to gain the commitment, the members must be willing to practice new skills. The skill development necessary to effectively use ROADS will take time. The time invested in this skill development will result in a higher success rate of gaining the commitment of prospective supporters. When that occurs, the organization will have created an effective new system that will benefit the organization for years to come.

APPENDIX

Gaining the Commitment Guide

-Checklist-

Name of Prospect

Date Process Initiated: Date Process Completed:

Date	Step	Description of Interaction	Type of Prospect* V/D/F/BOD	Additional Notes
	Relationship Building	1 2 3		
	Organized Prioritized Needs	1 2 3		
	Document Next Steps			
	Seek Feedback	Types of Feedback Systems to be Implemented with this supporter implemented		

*Type of Prospect:V=Volunteer/D=Donor/F=Funder/BOD=Board of Directors

Name of Individual Conducting Interview/Contact:

ABOUT THE AUTHOR

Bryan Nelson, MS, has over twenty-five years of management experience. His managerial experiences include educational administration, non-profit management, vice-president of his family's small business, and the owner of Vista Management Solutions, Inc. Additionally, Bryan has been an educational sales consultant for a small privately held sales company and for a billion dollar publicly traded sales company.

Mr. Nelson works as a management consultant for both non-profit and for-profit organizations. He understands the need for effective and efficient systems in gaining the commitment of supporters of non-profit organizations. *ROADS: The Non-Profit Quick Guide for Gaining the Commitment* was developed specifically to assist members of non-profit organizations in developing a systematic approach in gaining and then retaining the supporters every non-profit requires in today's world of shrinking resources and growing needs.

Made in the USA
Charleston, SC
16 November 2010